THE PACK

Coach Matt Deggs

Copyright © 2018 by Matt Deggs

All rights reserved. No portion of this book may be reproduced, stored in a retrieval system, or transmitted in any form or by any means—electronic, mechanical, photocopy, recording, scanning, or other—except for brief quotations in critical reviews or articles, without the prior written permission of the publisher.

ISBN-13: 978-1726312332
ISBN-10: 172631233X

To learn more about Coach Matt Deggs, visit
CoachDeggs.com

Pack Contents

The Pack Way
pg. 5

The Pack Mentality
pg. 23

4 Legs of the Wolf
pg. 47

Pack Absolutes
pg. 59

The 5 Phases
pg. 69

Plan of Attack
pg. 79

About the Author
pg. 95

THE PACK WAY

The most important thing that you will do is **build your team** and **create your culture**.

Peter Drucker, world famous renowned businessman and leader in the business community, said that...

"Culture eats strategy for breakfast."

That is the #1 component and #1 thing that we work on. A lot of people talk about The Pack and The Pack Offense and they want to know more, but it starts way before that... with our culture.

Recently, we brought in one of the nation's leading culture + team-building companies to visit us. This company works with teams all across the nation from the MLB to the NFL to Power 5 NCAA Teams. Basically, what this company did was take a look around and they evaluated our leadership and our culture.

After their evaluation, they found a couple of deficiencies in where we could improve – and we wanted that. We wanted that feedback of what we could do better. But, what I was super proud of and what really meant a lot to me was they told us that we were the **#1 culture that they had ever encountered**. I was just blown away that they would think that of us.

Culture doesn't take a day off. Culture is **24/7/365** and it's something that you have to work at every single day. It's exhausting. You've got to work at it with everything you've got.

The #1 thing that The Pack Way starts with is **clarity**...

Clarity = Focus

Without clarity, nobody knows the direction. Nobody knows where you're headed. You must have clarity.

A lack of clarity will actually at the moment of truth, when the rubber meets the road, make a coward out of you, because you do not understand the mission.

Here's the problem... Here's a trap that a lot of people fall into: **They think they have clarity, but they don't.** They can hear the beat in their head and they're wondering why no one else gets the song.

I'm going to play a song for you. I'm going to tap it out. <u>This</u> is our culture. I want you to understand our culture. I believe that you understand who we are, how we're going to do it, and where we're going. I believe you understand those things, but I want to play this out for you and I want you to name the song as soon as you know it. Here it goes...

"__ ____ ____ _____. __ ____ ____ _____."

Come on, tell me this song.

How come nobody is getting the song? That's where leaders get frustrated. **They see a lack of clarity in their mission and they don't know why.** It's because guys aren't grasping the mission. Even though you have a ton of knowledge and you work hard, that information may or may not be being disseminated the way that it should be. So when the song is played, when you have the beat in your head and nobody is getting the message and there's a total breakdown in communication, that falls upon <u>you</u> – **the leader** – because you set the tone, you create the clarity...

"___ ____ ____ _____. ___ ____ ____ _____."

Tell me the song. Nobody can get it. Here's the song. "We are the champions. We are the champions." That's the song. That's where the frustration is.

You may know what you want, but you have to demand what you want. You have to work at it every single day. Like I said, this is **24/7**. Culture never takes a day off. The #1 place it starts is with **clarity of mission**. You have to have clarity.

Now that everybody knows the song, and now that everybody can hear the beat, we're set. Now we're ready to go.

Clarity = Focus and if all of us in this organization have a laser beam focus as to where we're going, who we are, and how we're going to get there, then at that moment, we can do anything. It starts with clarity.

Then, the #1 thing after clarity that you have to do – and I'm going to talk about 4-5 of these things – is **you have to set the standard**. What do you stand for? There has to be a metaphorical bar. It is up to everybody in your organization to get above the bar. **There is no half-in or half-out.** You've got to be all the way in and you've got to get above the bar on a daily basis.

How do you get above the bar?

Well it starts for us with this… We talk a lot about **hope vs. expectation**. We are not allowed to use the word 'hope' inside of our organization.

For me, there are two kinds of hope. There is hope that is eternal… "I know the promise of things to come." Then there's a negative hope. This hope means that "I'm kind of prepared. I hope something happens."

Here's the difference between hoping and expecting… Hope means that "I've worked a little bit. I'm kind of prepared for it." Expectation? **Expectation means the blood and the sweat equity is in the bucket.** "I deserve success."

I tell our guys all the time here's the difference between the two. If I have a huge exam coming up and I spent 20 minutes the night before and then 10 minutes the day of prepping for this exam, then I'm kind of prepared. So, when I make a D or an F on that test then I'm just a little bit disappointed because I don't have any blood or sweat in the bucket. I've 'kind of' prepared. That is hope. "I hope I pass this test. I hope we win. I hope I get a hit. I hope I get this batter out."

Hope is not a strategy.

Hope is just a word that people use to insulate themselves in case of possible defeat. We tell our guys all the time, **"Know no such word. Prepare only for victory."** So when I hope for something, when I 'kind of' prepare and it doesn't work out for me, then I'm just a little bit disappointed. Life goes on and it's acceptable to me.

But flip the script.

When I go out and I get after it for this exam for 2 weeks leading up to it and I give it 30 minutes a night and I'm prepared for this exam, yet somehow someway it comes back and I've made a C on this exam. How do I feel now? The blood and the sweat and the tears and everything else is in the bucket. I've put them in. I deserve an A or a B on this exam. But I made a C. Well now I'm angry.

That's where we start our culture of getting above the bar, of living in a standard of hope vs. expectation. We ultimately surround ourselves with poor losers. We surround ourselves with guys that failure is just not an option for because they have prepared, they deserve and, they expect success.

The second part of setting our standard is energy.

Energy creates more energy.

That can work either way — with positive energy or negative energy. Energy will ultimately create more energy. That is the way that we operate here. In every single aspect of the program, in everything that we do, it's positive energy.

For instance: No matter the day, no matter what's going on, we could go through a 5-game losing streak, it doesn't matter. When I see one of our players or when they see each other, we're going to greet each other with a "How you doing?" The response now becomes an instant competition because they're going to shoot back at me when I say, "Hey Nick, how are you doing?" He's going to say "Great." Now it's up to me in creating energy to try and top that "Great." Then he's going to ask how I'm doing and I'm going to say "Awesome." Then we're going to shake hands and I'm going to try and crush his hand and he's going to try and crush my hand. Then there's going to be an argument ensuing over who crushed whose hand and **now we've created energy.**

In the same light, we've created a friendly competition that no matter what is going on around us we've taken that time to acknowledge each other, have great energy, great positive energy, and taken that time to compete at something. So now we're laughing, now we're smiling, and now we've surrounded ourselves with great energy.

Those two things right there are vital when you talk about setting a bar and raising the bar, living in the standard, when you look at hoping vs. expecting. **We expect in every aspect of this program. There is no hope.**

I don't answer with "I hope." "Are you going to pass that test this week?" "Well I hope I'm going to pass the test." Well right there you're telling me that you're not going to pass the test because you're telling me you're 'kind of' prepared.

Every answer that we give in this program is **expect**. When you combine that attitude with positive energy and love and care and empathy for your teammates and for your other coaches, then instantly you have raised the bar.

The second part of building a program and creating a culture is to create an identity.

Create one common pride or belief. Kids crave an identity. They crave to be a part of something bigger than themselves. We create that identity for them.

People crave an identity. People crave to be set apart. People crave to be part of something bigger than themselves. People crave to be elite. But, here's the thing about elite: **elite is not on sale**. You can't go to

Wal-Mart and buy elite. **You've got to earn elite.** So we start that with our identity.

Our identity is **The Pack** and **The Pack Mentality**.

From the time that we start recruiting a kid throughout the recruiting process until he gets here, they understand The Pack. They understand the identity that they're going to assume. Inside of The Pack, we set parameters around these kids, around these players, and we tell them where we see them right now and where we believe that they could be. Automatically, we start to create an identity.

Our two identities are The Pack and what we call **AAIT**...

The 4 pillars on which The Pack stands for:
Attitude
Approach
Intensity
Toughness

All of this, you have to keep in mind, is a crystal clear message chock full of clarity. Guys have to understand the mission. They have to understand who they are, where they're going, and how they're going to get there.

The 3rd thing inside of The Pack Way when we talk about creating a culture, building a team, building an organization, is **an organized, consistent and united message towards a common goal**.

A huge mistake that I see a lot of leaders make is that they're all over the map. One day you'll see a quote from this guy. Another day we're going in this direction. Another day this is who we are. You have to create an organized, united, consistent message. If we were only one thing in this program, I would choose to be organized and united. Organized and united can win at everything. Having a consistent message is key.

Every single one of our guys from the day that they get here is handed a binder. On this binder is a metaphorical mountain...

The metaphorical mountain can stand for a lot of things: goals in life, our goals as a team, something you might be facing right now, but that is our message from the get-go.

Who are we? We're The Pack.
Why are we here? It's to climb this mountain.

Along the way climbing this mountain, there are two key traits that we are going to pick up:

#1 - We're going to build well rounded men.

#2 - We're going to do that through AAIT:
    Attitude
    Approach
    Intensity
    Toughness

Inside of our binder is a calendar of everything that they will be involved in for the entire 9-10 months that they're here. With that is ownership and there is a consistent message inside of this binder. The only thing that we talk about from that day forward is how we are going to climb this mountain, and how we are going to do it.

It's clarity. Understanding these 3 things:

Who are we? The Pack.
Why are we here? To climb this mountain.
How are we going to do it? AAIT

That's clarity.

Along the way, we're going to pick up a lot of these traits that I'm talking about right now. We're going to pick up a lot of these things that you're going to need along your climb up this mountain. But the clarity of the entire mission is very simple.

We've created a culture of an organized, consistent, united message as to why we're here, who we are, and how we're going to do it. This is very, very important because if our message is all over the place, if there's a quote of the day, a quote of the week, and now we're going to hit this way or we're changing this pitch mechanic or this or that, there is no clarity and there is no singular mission.

The 4th thing inside of The Pack Way is you want to lead them to overachieve.

You want to build a program, an organization, a company, a team of overachievers in every area of their life. It's up to you as the leader and the team builder to lead them to overachieve.

These are the things that I consider leadership:

#1) Leadership is service.

In Mark 9:35, the disciples are arguing over who was going to lead after Jesus is gone. Jesus looks at them and he says, "If any of you want to be first, you must first be the very last and servant of all." Your job is to lead from the front and serve these guys. Don't tell somebody to do something. Show them how to do something. Show them how to do it.

It's the old "give a man a fish or teach him to fish" concept. I can make you do something but you're not going to learn it, and you're not going to have ownership in it, and you're not going to embrace it... or I can show you, and teach you, and you can learn from me as to how to do something, and you'll be able to do it the rest of your life and pass it down. **That's service.** That's leading from the front.

#2) Leadership is love.

I read a book by Joe Ehrmann called *InSideOut Coaching*, and I took this to heart. He said he had one job as the coach. This is what I tell our team every day. **My job is to love you. Your job is to love each other.** That's your only job. Love each other. My job in return is to love you. **Love is undefeated. Love conquers all.**

Everybody asks "How did you guys do what you did a year ago? How did you all get to that point when you come from a small mid-major and you only have this in comparison to all these other guys that have all of that?"

The answer is simple: **It was love.** We played for each other. We were all unafraid to crash and burn because of love. We had full hearts. We know we had the blood and sweat equity in the bucket. We deserved to win. So either way it went, we were thankful because we loved each other. You serve them and you love them.

#3) Motivate them.

Motivating, they say, is like showering. They recommend it daily. We motivate our guys to overachieve. You have to light that spark.

Think about this: one tiny spark, one cigarette thrown out the window can burn down a million acres. Why would you not light that spark every single day to get your guys motivated? We already know they have ability. They wouldn't be here if they didn't have ability. Now you get guys with ability to start to overachieve? The guy that has ability that doesn't overachieve is going to be good. But guys that have ability and overachieve in every aspect of their life? That guy is going to be <u>great</u>. You're going to build a great team.

#4) Never, ever, ever, be afraid to be embarrassed in front of your guys.

When we talk about leading your guys to overachieve – and this is so critical. It took me years and years and years to learn this as a coach, as a leader, as a man. **If you truly want to motivate and inspire them, let them see you.** Don't let them see the front that you might be putting on. Don't let them see the guy you think they want to see. Let them see <u>you</u>. Never be afraid to be embarrassed. Let them see you love. Let them see you laugh. Let them see you cry. Let them see you compete with them. **Let them see the real you.**

The mistake that's made a lot of times, especially in leadership, is guys build a false identity of themselves because their identity is wrapped in what they do instead of who they are. **When you learn to wrap your identity in who you are, instead of what you do, it is very liberating and very freeing.** Then you're allowed to be the real you and you're allowed to coach and lead unafraid. The only reason that you would be embarrassed ever in front of your team is because you're afraid of being exposed that there is a front being put on. But when your identity is wrapped up in serving these guys, loving these guys, motivating these guys, and showing them the real you, you are now free to be the leader that God made you to be.

#5) Get them to become the absolute best at the stuff nobody else cares about.

Celebrate every little thing. We don't look at the scoreboard. **The scoreboard is temporary.** We celebrate every little thing. The scoreboard, runs, hits, etc... are momentum related. **Momentum is temporary.** We celebrate eternal values: your work ethic, how early we get here *(If you're on time, you're late.)*, how late did we stay, how hard did we work? We celebrate those virtues. How hard did I get down the line? Our dugout will go crazy over a 6-pitch ground ball and the guy runs a 4.0 down the line because we control those things.

Celebrate every little thing. Be the best at the stuff that nobody else cares about. It's not cool anymore to work hard. We make it our mission to **outwork everybody**. It's not cool anymore to get here early, to be the first one here. It's not cool anymore to stay late. It's not cool anymore to play this game as hard as you can, to respect the game. We take pride in all those values, in all and we celebrate them. Here's the greatest part: All of those things are within our control. That's overachievement. That's going above and beyond.

The 5th and final thing inside of The Pack Way is cultivating an atmosphere of family and trust.

Within the cultivation of this atmosphere of family and trust is a sense of pride known only to those that have taken part, made an impact, and finished.

We accentuate that pride. We bring that out in our players... that you have taken part, you have made an impact, and you have finished. Those things are hard to do. You have got to celebrate those things and in doing so, in letting your guys see the real you, you're going to ultimately create this culture of family and trust.

But here's the deal: **You have got to be held to that same exact standard.** You yourself have got to be beyond reproach. You yourself have to take part daily, make a daily impact, and finish everything.

We have got a sign that hangs in our clubhouse. It says, **"If your presence doesn't make an impact your absence won't make a difference."**

You see how #4 and #5 kind of come together here? #4 and #5 come together when we talk about serving, loving, motivating, getting your guys to become the absolute best at the stuff nobody else cares about, and not being afraid to be embarrassed in front of your guys. You bring it together when you create an atmosphere of family and trust, cultivate that atmosphere, and you hold yourself accountable to those same measures.

When you've put in the work and you've created a culture, and that culture has now become a tradition, and that tradition bleeds itself all the way through the program out the door and into recruiting, so that your guys have an understanding of the culture, where the bar is, where the standard is, before they ever get here – **then you've got something special**.

Then, when you take that and you're not the one policing the culture anymore, your players are, now you've got a chance to dominate. Now you've got a chance to really win at a high level. And not just in baseball but in the game of life. This is one thing that we have been able to do that I believe sets us apart and has been incredible for us is from Day #1, from the time that our guys get on campus.

I'm going to tie a bow on this for you...

What we do in cultivating The Pack Way is use a little bit of the Navy SEAL model. I've been studying them since 1989. I was studying Navy SEALs before it was cool to study Navy SEALs. Since 1989, I've been looking at their leadership model and been patterning a lot of the stuff that I do personally as a coach, as a leader, as a mentor. I believe the Navy SEALs build the greatest leaders in the world. They build the greatest units in the world. It comes through their training.

What we do immediately upon our guys arriving here is make them a part of a **boat crew**.

We have three Boat Crews: **Boat Crew #1, Boat Crew #2, Boat Crew #3**.

This is vital when you talk about The Pack Way, when you talk about raising a bar, setting a standard, building an identity, having an organized and united message, getting guys to overachieve, and then cultivating that atmosphere of family and trust. These Boat Crews have leaders emerge out of them. Inside of the three Boat Crews, I have assistant coaches that are over each Boat Crew. Underneath them is what we call a **Boat Crew Leader**. That is an emerging leader on our ball club. Their sole purpose is to lead their Boat Crew.

Underneath them is everybody else in their Boat Crew and everybody else is attached to what we call a **'swim buddy'**. I am solely responsible to my swim buddy in every phase of what we do - from the classroom to the weight room to off the field to community service.

My sole responsibility from the time I get here is not to the whole team. It's to my swim buddy.

After that, it's to my Boat Crew.

After that, it's to the team.

So our tradition and our standards and everything that we stand for is passed down through our players. The swim buddies report to each other, who report to their Boat Crew, who report to their leader, who report to that assistant coach, who ultimately comes to me.

That is a system of discipline, accountability, and trust in every single thing that we do.

I will tell you this. It's something that I'm proud of. I think it's been 2 ½ years since we've even had somebody show up late for something. There have been no issues, no discipline issues, no anything.

The culture is passed down through these kids into their swim buddies, into their Boat Crews. Information is disseminated from me to the assistant coach to the Boat Crew leader and then these kids will have to learn how to communicate and they have to learn to put themselves aside and they have to learn to take care of each other.

If my responsibility is to my swim buddy first, and then to my Boat Crew and my Boat Crew leader, and then to the whole team - then for me personally, I fit in last in that equation. So I'm learning to serve. I'm learning to love. I'm learning to motivate. I have to be the real me. I'm becoming a part of a family that's only known to those who have taken part.

THE PACK MENTALITY

I've done more speaking across the country for the past 10 years on this topic than any other topics that we're going to talk about...

This is really the nuts and bolts and what everybody likes to talk about.

I want to give you a little bit of background of how The Pack come about. The Pack was born in the summer of 2006. I was at Texas A&M at the time. I had just come from the University of Arkansas. I was there with my best buddy, Rob Childress, who was and still is the head coach at A&M. I was the hitting coach and recruiting coordinator. We had both experienced great success at the University of Nebraska and the University of Arkansas prior to coming to Texas A&M.

2006 was our first season together. I'm thinking to myself, *"This is going to be easy."* The Lord had other plans. I got humbled pretty good that year from the standpoint of wins and losses and how we produced as an offense. It was very frustrating for me in the fact that I take stuff like that personally. I think any coach takes numbers, or wins and losses, personally.

I spent an entire summer really thinking to myself, "Where did this go wrong?" I think this is a trap that a lot of us fall into as coaches. I knew the way that I had always coached, so I knew what I was doing. It's kind of like in Chapter 1 when we talk about The Pack Way and it starts with what when building a culture?

It starts with **clarity**.

The point that I'm making right here is that I knew the way that I coached, but I had never written it down.

I had never defined it.

I had never put parameters on the way I coached or put an expectation to the way I coached. It took me getting knocked on my butt and really, really humbled as a hitting coach going through that 2006 season. I was determined to make sure that the season was not going to be in vain. I was determined that I was going to learn from that season.

As a guy that was running the offense there and coaching the hitters, I just could never get the players to buy-in during that 2006 season. We had tremendous success at Texarkana Junior College and at the University of Arkansas offensively.

We were very dynamic with speed and strength, what I call Thunder and Lightning... but there was no rhyme or reason to it. There was no definition to it. There was no definitive system. It took me going to A&M thinking, "Here we go. We're going to just do the same things that we had been doing," and I got knocked right on my butt that first year in 2006. This was weighing on me as I was out on the road recruiting that summer. Everywhere I went, that was all that was on my mind.

It wasn't until I took a night off. I was at the house, and I was watching one of the nature-wildlife channels, and literally (You're not going to believe me, but literally...), there was a documentary on a pack of wolves.

At that instant I had that "Aha" moment.

I had that light bulb moment of "That's it."

I started really watching this documentary.

The interesting part about wolves is they all have a job. They all have a duty. They all have a function. In order to survive in the wild, this pack of wolves has to function together. You have alpha wolves, beta wolves, caretaker wolves, scout wolves, hunter wolves, protective wolves. They <u>all</u> have a job.

The most interesting part I learned through this documentary was:

There's really and truly no such thing as a lone wolf.

Lone wolves go off and die. When you equate that to a team, you equate that to a business, you equate it to an organization, any unit that is responsible for completing a task or a job, that is so very true. There is no room, there is no place, for a lone wolf.

So that is how The Pack was born in 2006.

Now that you have the backstory, I want to talk about **The Pack Mentality**. This is where we start to tie in our identity...

Who are we? <u>We are *The Pack*</u>.

"For the strength of the pack is the wolf, but the strength of the wolf is the pack."

In our mind, in our eyes, nothing ever comes before team. Ever. That is at the essence. That is the core. If we finished talking right now, that is the one core that you have to take away from this:

NOTHING COMES BEFORE TEAM.

"For the strength of the pack is the wolf..."

Yes, we need you. We need your individuality. We need your personality. We need your skill set.

That is how we do what we do offensively (and not just offensively). This goes for a group of hitters. This goes for a group of pitchers. This goes for an entire team. This goes for a business, a company, a corporation.

We need you to do your job. We love your skill set. We love your personality. We covet those things. But understand this: You cannot do anything without the help of others.

We have a saying around here:

"If we don't care who gets the credit, we can do incredible things."

Our teams understand this right up front. It's just the nature of where we're at. It's the nature of being a David in a land full of Goliaths. That alone left at our own disposal, we are probably (including myself) very, very, very ordinary. But together as one, as one team or one pack, one family, we can be pretty extraordinary.

As long as we don't care who gets the credit, we can do amazing things. That is the essence of **The Pack**.

See this image in your mind as you read this… I want you to visualize this.

It's a buffalo. Around this buffalo are 9 wolves. I want you to ask yourself a question…

How are those 9 wolves going to take down that buffalo?

You're probably going to come to the same conclusion as me... It's not going to be one individual wolf going to attack that buffalo. If one wolf jumps in and goes after that buffalo, what's going to happen to that wolf? He's going to get gored in short order and he's going to die. That is what happens when people put themselves in front of the business, the organization, the corporation, or the team. They go off and they die.

To take down that buffalo, **you have to function together**. This is what we use to paint a picture for anything that we might be doing. It is this metaphorical buffalo...

That buffalo could be Omaha.

That buffalo could be a Friday-night starter.

That buffalo could be a nasty lineup you're facing.

That buffalo represents any challenge that you are facing in your life today.

How are you with your unit/team/family/organization (whatever it might be)... How are you going to take down that buffalo?

You will only come to one answer because 1-on-1 you're no match. You are no match.

You get humbled real quick when you think you can do anything without the help of others.

Once you humble yourself to that fact, then you are free to do your job.

You will take down that buffalo eventually if you work as a pack and you do your job. It's not going to be pretty. Our guys understand that going in. They understand you're going to come out of this confrontation bloodied, beat up, battered, bruised. But ultimately, I promise you this: **We will surround and we will take down that buffalo because we won't stop coming**.

That's the thing about this. We're not walking with a safety net here. Our survival depends on taking down this buffalo so we won't stop coming. It will be wave after wave, one guy after the next. You might wear an 0-for-4.

But you might be the guy that draws that big walk too, that scores a winning run. You might wear a 1-for-5, but that 1 was a 2-out knock. You might have 3 punches, but you wore a huge hit by pitch.

Just keep coming.

Just keep surrounding, doing your job, and ultimately, we will take down that buffalo and it will go down with a resounding thud. That is **The Pack.**

Inside of The Pack we stand upon – and this is very, very important – an organized and consistent message: **AAIT**.

Attitude, **A**pproach, **I**ntensity, and **T**oughness.

Those are the 4 pillars on which we stand, and you don't have **The Pack** without them.

Attitude for us is a supreme confidence in our ability to win in any circumstance in any situation.

At the end of the day, I expect to win in everything that I do. I don't hope to win. I expect to win. Everything for us inside of **The Pack** is a competition with the end result being an expectation to win. In everything. We talked about it in The Pack Way of creating a culture of **hope vs. expectation**. Hope meaning I'm kind of prepared. Expectation meaning the blood and sweat is in the bucket. I deserve to win. That is the way that I will carry myself in every situation that I'm in, and that is what we instill in our guys.

If it's an at-bat... If I'm in the box, I expect to win. I expect to win every pitch. Am I going to? No. But I will have an extremely short memory, and I will be the same dude every day, and you will not deter me from expecting to win in anything I do.

If I'm playing a game of Monopoly against you right now, you know what? I expect to win.

If it's a pickup basketball game, I expect to win.

If it's a game of cards, I expect to win.

If I'm in the same class as you, I expect to make better grades than you.

If we're in the weight room, I'm going to out work you because of an expectation to beat you.

These 4 pillars have to be ingrained in your guys. They're not going to come in understanding all four of these. They're not going to be able to come in and pull off all four of these initially. So it is up to you to put them in situations where you can ingrain these four pillars into your guys.

Attitude is a perception. Why else would a wolf show you his fangs? A wolf will show you his fangs to let you know that this is about to go down and you need to back up.

Attitude is no different. It is a perception. It is a belief.

That belief will ultimately become your reality as to what's about to happen. It's not arrogance. It's expectation. We demand that our kids, in every phase of their life, expect to win.

At the end of the day, that's what this country was founded on – competition and winning.

We expect to win.

The second pillar is **Approach**: my job, duty, or function at any given time within the confines of The Pack or the team.

Who am I? How do I go about my business? I have to have an understanding of who I am. I ask myself one question every single day: **What can I do today to help us win a championship?**

I tell our guys all the time, "You know what, if our janitor is on vacation for two weeks, and he needs somebody to fill in for him and there's nobody to fill in, I will fill in for the janitor. In order to make sure that this place is clean, this place is presentable, and this place looks first class I will step in for him because on this day to help us win a championship my job is to fill in for our custodian. I will do that."

Nobody in this organization is above doing any job. Any job. Everybody in this organization (myself included) is on equal footing. From the custodian to the head coach and everybody in between, we all have a job, duty, or function to do, and we will make the absolute least – and this is key – **we will make the absolute least feel like the most important.** This is key to a winning culture. There is no hierarchy here. There is nobody above anybody else. We all at the end of the day have a job, duty, or function to pull off. Just do your job, whatever that might be.

The interesting part about The Pack is this when we talk about approach: **Who am I and how do I go about my business?** Even in the initial recruiting process we tell guys where we see them fit inside of The Pack. We tell guys this so there is already an understanding when you come in of what your job is going to be.

Back to that organized and united, consistent message – **everybody understands their job.** With that, everybody else also understands your job. This is key because when everybody else understands your job, now there's accountability to it. When your team holds the team accountable for doing their job, you've got a chance.

So we've got Attitude, we've got Approach, and the third pillar is this: **Intensity**

Intensity is our best tool by far. I talked about it in an earlier video. **Alone we'd be ordinary, but together we're extraordinary.** Intensity allows us to overachieve. Intensity is our love for the challenge of competition. We get guys that love to compete. In everything they do, they love to compete. Our love for the challenge of competition is intensity. We get behind that. We play the game with our hair on fire. We celebrate every little bitty small thing. We play this game with passion and we celebrate that. **Intensity can truly allow you to overachieve.**

Here's a for instance: If you take two guys and they're both of the same ability level, and you put these two guys against each other – in whatever the competition might be – and the entire team gets around this guy and they cheer for him and they pull for him and they have pertinent talk for this guy and this other guy is left all on his own, who is going to win that confrontation?

It's going to be the guy that his teammates get behind him with intensity because that that guy is not going to let his teammates down. Intensity will allow you to overachieve.

But this is the greatest thing about intensity: **Intensity, in it's purest definition, in its purest form, means wave after wave after wave.** Imagine going down to the Galveston sea wall and looking out into the Gulf. What's going to happen all day?

Wave after wave after wave. At the essence, at the core of who The Pack is, our guys are conditioned to never stop coming after you. That's why we hit, that's why we score – because we respond.

The most important thing you'll ever do in your life is get back up and respond.

Stay off results.
Stay on to each other.
Respond.

With intensity you might get this guy, you might get this guy, you might get this guy -- but oh, here comes this guy, and it's just not going to stop. You will have to kill us to stop us. You have to condition your guys to that mindset.

That's intensity.
Intensity is our best tool.
It allows us to overachieve.

The 4th pillar is **Toughness**. (Toughness is the hardest to acquire.) Nobody is going to show up truly having toughness because it takes having gone through some type of adversity to acquire toughness.

Adversity doesn't make you a man. What adversity does is it exposes, for everybody to see, where you're at as a man.

Everybody is going to go through adversity in their life. Everybody is going to wear that 0-10, and they're going to have to sit out three games. Everybody is going to have a period where they flunk a biology test or a girlfriend breaks up with them, or maybe it all comes together. That in itself is not going to make you a man. It's only going to expose where you're at as a man for all your teammates to see, for your entire organization to see, and it will at that instant give you a chance to respond.

The most important thing you'll ever do in your life is get back up.

Embrace the grind and continue to just keep coming.

If a guy can do that, he's got toughness.

That's toughness. **Our definition of toughness is your Attitude, your Approach, and your Intensity in the midst of adversity.** We want to see how you respond to that adversity. It's not the adversity itself that's going to make you. It's how you respond to that adversity. Your Attitude, your Approach, and your Intensity in the midst of that adversity will define who you are. It will define the name on the back of your jersey for everybody to see.

Once you have Attitude and you have Approach and you have started to acquire Intensity and Toughness, what I have found is this:

You get two byproducts of those four traits. You start to see **Aggressors** and you start to see **Competitors**.

9 out of 10 times, the aggressor. An aggressor for us is the guy that can play the game with the freedom of the fear of consequence. This guy is not going to tiptoe. This guy is unafraid to crash and burn in anything he does. Why would he be unafraid to crash and burn?

Generally, guys are unafraid to crash and burn when their hearts are full of love, and they're prepared and there is clarity of mission. But if there is no clarity of mission, there's no preparedness, and their hearts are not full of love, they will be afraid to crash and burn. They're going to want to tiptoe because they're afraid to lose.

We are looking for the guys that play the game with the freedom of the fear of consequence in everything we do.

They play fast, hard, and lose, and they have a ball doing it. They play with intensity.

A competitor for us, the second byproduct, is a guy that simply hates losing more than he enjoys winning. Failure is just not an option. Is it going to happen? Yeah… but it's not an option. Like I said earlier, he is going to have a short memory. He is going to be the same guy every single day. He'll learn from it. He's not going to dwell on it and he's going to move on. That's a competitor. A guy that hates losing more than he enjoys winning but has the ability to move on from it. He's not stuck in the things that happened in the past.

So those are the 4 pillars: **Attitude, Approach, Intensity, and Toughness**. Without those there is no Pack. After you obtain those 4 pillars, you're hunting the two byproducts – **Aggressors** and **Competitors**.

Within The Pack, we set parameters around our guys from the get go.

We have four categories inside of The Pack Offense:
- **Runners**
- **Hitters**
- **Bombers**
- **Ballplayers**

Joe Torre said this about Derek Jeter, and I really took this to heart when I saw this:

"When Derek Jeter learned his limits, when he learned who he was, he became limitless."

Remember me talking about the 2nd Pillar, Approach? **You have to teach guys who they are.** No two players are exactly alike. That's why we've got 4 categories. Everybody can fit into one of these 4 categories. Once they do fit into one of these 4 categories, you set parameters around them.

Well, what do these parameters really mean? Really and truly, what we're telling you is who we believe you are and what our expectation for your job is within that category?

When I explain this, I want you to put yourself back in that focus of that metaphorical buffalo and that buffalo is surrounded by nine wolves...

With **Runners**, it's pretty self-explanatory... Runners are guys that have run **6.6 second 60-yard dashes** or better and have the **ability to extend at bats**.

To even meet our criteria, this runner has got to run at 6.6 seconds or better. He's got to be able to handle the bat. He's got to be able to shorten the field for us. He's got to have the heart to run. A lot of guys are fast, but very few guys have the heart to run. Going back to the ole' crash and burn thing again, you've got to have the heart to run. You've got to have the guts of a cat burglar to be a runner for us.

Let's think about that metaphorical picture that we drew up. We've got a runner. This is what I want you to hear. A runner, his sole job is to be a distraction. We want that buffalo's eyes to come off of the rest of us and go on to who? Go on to that runner. That's what runners do for us.

Here's the most beautiful part about The Pack... We explain it to guys before we ever get them. We coach no one guy the same. We coach The Pack based off of who they are in our base running, in our BP, in our early work, in the way we build a lineup, in the way that we recruit. The entire thing is built and based upon accentuating the personalities and the traits of these four categories that I'm going through right now. This transcends just a category. This goes into every part of our program.

You're a runner? Okay, this is what you have today in practice. This is your early work. This is your baserunning. This is what your BP will look like, and this is your job: extend at bats, cut down strike outs, be a distraction, reach base. The #1 thing that he will do is **reach base**. Have a short game. Have the heart to be a distraction. That's a runner. We will bring that out in this player in everything that we do with him.

Hitters are the most dynamic players that we have on the ball club. Hitters are always going to be your guys that have the best blend of speed and strength.

Hitters are on the biggest scholarships. Hitters generally are your guys that are going to go on and play for a paycheck and have a chance to make it to the big leagues. They're your most dynamic players.

This is why they're hard to find. It's hard to find a team full of hitters. Hitters have to have the ability to play inside of all four categories. There's got to be a little runner to them. There's got to be a lot of hitter to them. There's got to be a little bomber to them. There's got to be a little ball player to them. So, they are actually held accountable to playing inside of all four categories.

The way that we define these categories, and the way we put them together is like this:

I want you to think of a sliding scale...

The more power you have, the slower your foot speed can be.

The less power you have, the higher your foot speed better be.

To become a hitter for us, the first criteria is this: You've got to be a 6.8 second runner or better. You've got to have strength from your fingertips to your elbows. You've got to have 20+ double potential. You've got to have a knack for producing runs.

At the end of the day, that's truly what a hitter is going to do. He is a run producer. He has a knack for consistent hard contact and big hits, but at the end of the day, he is a run producer.

By being a distraction, by being able to get big hits, by being able to run the ball out of the ballpark, and by being able to execute, this guy has the ability to play inside of all four categories. That for us is a hitter. Those guys are hard to find. If you find one, you better covet him because this guy has a chance to be super, super, dynamic inside of your offense. If you can ever build a lineup of all hitters, you're going to be deadly.

Once again, I want you to stay in this frame of mind for me. When we look back and think about that metaphorical buffalo and about this pack of wolves having to work together to take down this buffalo so that they can eat (or so that you can win)... If a runner is a distraction, then the hitter is a guy that once that buffalo is distracted is going in there looking to inflict damage.

Bombers are self-explanatory. They're big physical guys that are there to be a presence in the lineup. I hit bombers in group 2 of BP. I'll have an entire group of bombers because they're there to be a presence. I need them to be not just a presence but a perception. I need them to be a distraction to the other team as well, and that's why they're hitting in group two of BP.

Why group two of BP?
That's about the time the other team shows up.

When the other team shows up, what I want them to perceive are balls going out of the ballpark. When in reality, this bomber, if he's in the lineup, may hit 7, 8, or 9 for us, but the opposing team is having to prepare for this bomber five batters out because of what they have already seen with their own eyes. They have one job and that's to challenge the fence on every swing. If a runner is shortening the field, then a bomber is lengthening the field.

Everybody is working together within The Pack. You have a distraction. You have a run producer. Now you have this perception in this bomber. He may hurt you. He may not. I don't know. But you've already perceived the danger when you walked in the ballpark and saw him hit. Those are bombers. Bombers are physical guys with lots of strength at contact. They have the ability to lengthen the ballpark with real 10-20+ jack potential.

The last category for us inside of The Pack – and this is where 99.999% of the population of the Earth would fit in, and I know it's where I would have been – is a **Ball Player**.

Ballplayers are the backbone of our program. Ballplayers are not the fastest, the biggest or the strongest. They're not on the biggest scholarships by any means. But you have to have them. **Ballplayers push you.** Whereas they might not be the strongest, fastest, most gifted, a lot of these guys are jack-of-all-trades. A lot of these guys are very adept defensively. A lot of these guys are very heady players. A lot of these guys are really good bat handlers.

The way I want you to think about a ballplayer in terms of taking down this buffalo is in this respect. We call our ball players cannon fodder and they know this. Ballplayers for us know this, and by knowing this, they take a tremendous amount of pride in this. When we're taking down this buffalo, ballplayers are expendable.

Well what do I mean by expendable? The ultimate goal of a ballplayer is to be adept defensively and to execute on demand.

Ballplayers at bats for us are expendable. These are your guys that will squeeze. These are the guys wearing the bulk of your hit by pitches. These are your hit and run guys. These are your guys that may take a strike to two strikes. These guys are going to extend real quick innings by taking pitches. These guys are going to sacrifice bunt, and they take a tremendous amount of pride in all of these things.

The #1 thing that makes The Pack go is the ability to take pride in doing your job and sacrificing for a brother.

"There is no greater honor than to sacrifice for a brother." -John 15:13

Our guys don't complain about this. Our guys are saying, *"Coach pick me. You've got a dirty job? I'll do it."* But you have to accentuate this, you have to praise this, and you have to bring this out in your ball club.

So those are the four categories: **Runners, Hitters, Bombers, Ballplayers**. They all have a job, duty, and function and they all have to work together in order to take down that buffalo. You have to train and you have to develop them based off of who they are as players with the God-given ability that they have.

There is no one size fits all. There is no cookie cutter practice plan and there is no one practice plan for everybody for the sake of efficiency. If you are truly into development, then you will coach and mold and develop these young players based off the abilities that they have. You won't let them lie to themselves. They will understand where you see them.

We tell these kids who they are, we put the parameters around them, and then we demand they prepare that way and do their job that way for the benefit of the team. Then, we water them, we feed them, we nurture them, and we watch them grow into the player that they were made to be.

Along the way you're going to win a lot of games doing this. You're going to have a lot of fun. You're going to build a very, very, very dynamic team.

THE 4 LEGS OF THE WOLF

I want to tie having an organized, united, consistent message within your culture with feeding the 4 Legs of the Wolf.

There is no wolf that is productive that has three legs, that has two legs, that has one leg. He has four healthy, productive legs. The legs feed that wolf. This is our WHY. This is our organized message. There are four parts to the message that feeds the 4 Legs of the Wolf.

It starts with #1 – our **Vision**.

For me, it's really simple. I've always been this way growing up – an underdog, an overachiever, a grinder. In our society today, the word *"grind"* is very prevalent. We've got our own definition for grind. For us, **"to grind" is a continual pursuit to overachieve in any and all situations using the gifts that God gave you in order to obtain a desired outcome**.

When you look at the 4 Legs of the Wolf, they all go towards a desired outcome. You have to overachieve to get to that point of that desired outcome.

If you can see it in your mind's eye and if you can believe it in your heart, and then, you can wake up with that pilot light lit in your belly and wake up every morning, punch that card, and go outwork everybody, then **at that moment you're in the business of the impossible**.

All things will be possible for you, and I truly believe you can go get and obtain what you're looking for. That's our vision.

Our vision is very, very clear. It's 40+ wins every year. It's a conference championship. It's a conference tournament championship. It's an NCAA Regional championship. It's the opportunity, collectively as a university, as a program, as a team, as a community, to one day walk through the Gates of Omaha together.

That's our vision and our vision never waivers. Remember going back to that little word we talked about in The Pack Way: **Clarity**. Everybody understands the vision. We all can see it. We all believe it. We all work extremely hard for it.

The second leg of the wolf is our **Mission**.

The mission is the only promise that we as coaches/leaders make to you the player. It starts in the recruiting process. It's the only promise that we make. We're not going to promise you the biggest scholarship. We're not going to promise you that you're going to play. We're not going to promise you a certain locker. We're not going to promise you your number. You will absolutely work and earn everything you get here. But we do promise you this:

We work for you.

Inside of this mission, there are four things that I guarantee that we're going to do for you...

First and foremost is this: **When Mom and Dad drop you off, we are going to pick up in your development as a man.** That's most important with us. This is threefold for us. It's mind, body, spirit. We're going to develop you into a well-rounded man. We already know you can play baseball. We want to develop you into a well-rounded man that is ready to go out and be a productive member in the community and be a great husband, a great father, a great business owner, a great professional, a great professional baseball player... whatever it might be.

Your identity is <u>not</u> wrapped into and defined by what you do. Instead, it is wrapped into who you are, and who we want you to become is a well-rounded man ready to go out and make a difference in your community. That's our first promise. We'll develop you as a man.

The second part of our mission is that **we're going to develop you as a player**. God gave you the ability. We're going to get it out of you. We're going to push. We're going to prod. We're going to prompt. We're going to put parameters around you going back to The Pack. We're going to identify your skill set. We're going to tell you your job and define that job for you. We're going to give you our expectation of you. Like I said with The Pack Mentality, we're going to nurture you, we're going to water you, and like a tree coming up out of the ground, we're going to watch you grow. We're going to watch you develop into the player that God intended you to be with the ability that he gave you.

So that's the first two parts of our mission: develop you as a man (mind, body spirit) and developing you as a player, teaching you an understanding of who you are and how you need to go about your business in order to become the best player that you can be.

I believe that this is something that we've done as well as anybody over the past several years… especially coming from schools that maybe aren't the biggest schools or have the most resources or aren't able to attract the most talented guys.

We have to find guys that are what we call **OKG**s… **our kind of guys**. Guys that fit what we do. Then we have to develop them as men and we have to develop them as players. We have to be unwavering in that process.

You have to fit what we do athletically. Offensively, if you're a guy that has arm action and you have some speed and strength but you're still a little bit raw at the game, that's great. We'll take you.

You like to play the game hard and you have a passion for the game? We're going to take you.

On the bump, if you're a guy that can locate a fastball, has the makings of an out pitch, can field his position, hold runners, wants the ball, likes to compete… That's a guy that we're going to be interested in. That's a guy that we're going to try to get.

But above and beyond those things, you have to be a guy that plays the game hard, plays the game with passion, loves to get after it, loves his teammates, and loves to work. If you have those characteristics and abilities, then our mission is to develop that.

The third part of our mission is to **make sure that you're on track to graduate and that you do receive that degree**. We're going to see it through until you receive that degree. That degree is not just an ordinary key. That degree is a master key. A master key doesn't just open that door or maybe that door. A master key opens up every single door. Along with the degree, what you are getting is an incredible network, an incredible opportunity to open doors for the rest of your life. It's not so much necessarily about the GPA that you finished with as much as the ability to show everyone that you started something and you completed something and you were able to network along the process. At that point, you have the ability to open up every door for the rest of your life.

The 4th part of that mission for us as coaches is that **we're going to win championship rings together**. I believe that winning is a vital part of the experience in your development as a man, in your development as a player, and even in your mission towards getting that degree. We're going to win championship rings together. Over the course of my career, we've been very blessed in the fact that this promise (our mission) has come true for every player that we've ever had at some point during their time with us.

Rings are something that everybody wants but it's last in our coaches' mission. It's last in the promise that we make you. It's last because those things are fleeting. It's last because those things are temporary.

Inside of our mission as coaches, what we want to teach are eternal values — hard work, dedication, loyalty, commitment. It starts with the development of the man and then the development of the player, making sure that you see something through from start to finish, and then winning championship rings.

I've got a box full of rings at home. I don't wear them. Why? Because I've got the memories of those teams. I've got the memories of those players. I've got the memories of those ball clubs right here with me. A ring is something that's fleeting. Now I'm very honored and proud to have those rings but what truly means something is seeing these players go from kids to well-rounded men and going from raw ballplayers to guys that are developed.

We've had several guys over the course of my career that didn't play for their high school but went on to play for a paycheck. I like to think that we were a part of that developmental process as a man and as a player. Then when they walk across that stage and get that degree, and I see that they've gotten that master key that's going to unlock every door for the rest of their life, that makes it all worth it. The cherry on top is the championship ring.

You can't jump the process and preach championship rings without the development as a man, as a player, and making sure they're on track to graduate. You have to be well rounded and well thought out and have perspective in every single thing that you do.

The third leg of the wolf is our **expectation**.

We map it out for every kid in this program. We're not result-oriented coaches. What I mean by that is this: We're not going to ask you to come in here and hit .350 or pitch it at a 2.00 ERA or hit 10 jacks or have a 3:10 strikeout to walk ratio in the fall of your freshman year or in the fall of your junior college transfer year because those are results and those things are fleeting and those things are very temporary. You don't have control over all of those things all the time.

We tell our guys all the time one thing:

Results are temporary. Your commitment to team and your commitment to each other is forever.

We don't make decisions based off of pure results. We have an expectation. This is all part of our consistent, united, organized message that we're giving these guys. If they can check these boxes of our expectation, then they can play here.

The first box is this for us: **We want you to come in here and show mastery of what we call The 3 M's.**

What are the three M's? It starts for us with this:

Manage your time/get organized.

That's our first expectation. The biggest mistake that guys make when they get here or while they're here is a lack of time management and a lack of organization. Manage your time. Write it down. Put it on the calendar. Get organized in every phase of your life. That's the first M.

The second M is:

Master your routine.

There is no great professional, businessman, or great leader that does not manage his or her time and is not organized and doesn't have a routine that is mastered. There's not one. **All successful people manage time and master a routine.**

Losers never have time.
Winners make time.

You know the guy…
"Hey, let's go lift weights."
"I ain't got time."

"Hey you want to study for this test?"
"I'm out of time."

That's a losing mentality.
Winners make time.

"Yeah I'm busy man, give me one minute and I'll be there." Winners make time to get it done.

There are no great, successful people, leaders, CEOs, managers, you name it… that don't manage their time or don't have a successful routine. We demand that you start to manage your time, get organized, and master your routine. That routine is different for everybody. You have your own routine wherever you're at, whatever school, whatever business, whatever you might be in. You have your own routine, but you must demand that your routine is mastered.

The mastery of a routine equals confidence, and **when you have confidence, all things are possible.** Once I've started to manage that time and master that routine, now I can begin to…

Make a positive impact.

I talked about it in an earlier…

If your presence doesn't make a positive impact, nobody is going to remember you in your absence… Nobody.

The second part of that expectation is this: **You carry 15+ credit hours in school.** You're here to get a degree. We demand you carry 15+ hours, then we're looking for guys that carry a 3.0 GPA or better. Our team GPA is almost always around a 3.3 so we demand that our guys carry a

3.0 or better or that they're working towards it. There are some guys that just aren't going to get there, but they've got to be working towards it.

We incentivize our guys. It's basic economics 101. If you see anybody on our team that has long hair or facial hair or a mustache, that guy has a 3.0 or better.

Logic has kind of flipped upside-down with us. If you see one of our guys that is clean cut + clean shaven, that guy is probably not getting it done in the classroom. We incentivize our guys to get it done in the classroom. It gives them a little reward. It gives them a little something to be working towards.

The next part of our expectation is that **we serve our community**.

To whom much is given, much is required.

We truly believe in giving back to our community, so we put it on all of us to serve our community. We are here to make a positive impact in our community.

The last part of our expectation is this:

You practice hard, play hard, compete, and you love your teammates.

The most beautiful part of our expectation for our guys is this: <u>none of this stuff that I mentioned takes any talent.</u> It just takes a lot of **want** to.

Nowhere did I say I need you to hit .400. Nowhere did I say I need your ERA to be at a 1.5. Nowhere did I say you need to field .990.

A lot of times those things are not in your control. What I did say in essence is that **I want you to become absolutely great at the things that are in your control**.

The three M's are in your control. Carrying 15 hours? Maintaining a 3.0 or higher? Serving your community? That stuff is in your control. Practicing hard, playing hard, loving your teammates and competing? You control those things. None of those things take any talent… just a lot of fire, desire, and want to.

The fourth leg of the wolf is **Our Standard**.

Our standard hangs right outside our clubhouse. We don't have a rule book. We don't have a policy manual. What we live by is a standard. The standard is an acronym and it looks like this:

All things are possible.
We bring energy.
I like to help, I like to serve.
No excuses.
Never out of the fight.
EXPECT.
Ready to work, ready to lead.

If you look at it, it spells out **A WINNER.** If you can live inside of that standard, if you can get above the bar on a daily basis, there's not going to be any problems.

We haven't had a guy late to something in 3 years.

There are no rules.
There is a standard.

We expect you to live inside of our standard. The players are the ones that police this and hold each other accountable. At the bottom of the standard, it says that **Our commitment to this standard will only run as deep as our belief as to where we're going**. In other words, *I'll only be committed as deep as I believe.*

If you truly believe that with every fabric of your being, you're going to be committed and you're going to make Omaha-type decisions. You're going to make team-type decisions. You're going to make great decisions – personal, family, business-oriented, or otherwise.

Great decisions are made by very confident people who have a ton of belief in themselves followed only by more belief in something bigger than themselves.

That's team.
Nothing comes before team.

THE PACK ABSOLUTES

When talking about The Pack Absolutes, we begin to tie in overachievement in the sense of leading guys to overachieve and creating a culture of overachievers.

The beautiful part about The Pack is it accentuates and brings out guys' personal skills and personalities. Remember, every guy in the pack has a different job, duty, or function. Every guy is uniquely different inside of The Pack.

The Pack Absolutes kind of flip that script. This is the part of The Pack that everybody does <u>the exact same way</u>.

If you want to play for us and if you want to be a productive pack member, you have to be able to uphold, understand and live The Pack Absolutes. The Pack Absolutes for us are about ***being the absolute best at the stuff nobody else cares about***. We take a tremendous amount of pride in staying off the scoreboard and controlling what we can control.

Let's talk about some of the things that you don't control in this game. You don't control the lineup. You don't control the media. You don't control message boards. You don't control weather. You don't control your opponent. You don't control umpires. **A huge mistake that a lot of teams and leaders make is getting into**

the business of trying to control what they can't control. On the flip side of that, we want to be really rock solid at what we do control.

Some of the things that we control: our attitude, our effort, how we get on and off the field, our appearance, our love for each other, our support for each other, how we play the game, how we respect the game, how we serve, how we lead... All of these things are in our control. We set out to become the absolute best at the stuff nobody else cares about and do an incredible job at what we can control. This is the basis of The Pack Absolutes, and I want to go through each one of them and explain how important they are to us.

I want you to think about each one of these absolutes and how your ball club or your team or your organization can celebrate the little things. When you celebrate the little things, it becomes one gigantic thing, and it instills a huge sense of pride that's only known to the guys that have taken part in it.

The first Pack Absolute for us is:

Intensity is our best tool.
A carpenter wouldn't leave home without his hammer or his saw or his level. Intensity is something that travels. We can never leave home without intensity. It is our best tool. If you remember back to The Pack Mentality when I talked about the 4 pillars – Intensity will allow you and your ball club or organization to overachieve.

Intensity is by far our best tool. We are not skilled or good enough to leave home and play without passion, to play without emotion, to play without our hair on fire. **If there's ever a day where we decide to leave our best tool, to leave our hammer at the house, we will get beat.** So we have an understanding before we do anything that the #1 Pack Absolute on this ball club is that intensity is our best tool and it allows us to overachieve.

Intensity in its purest form meaning wave after wave after wave. It allows us to respond and gives us the ability to keep coming because intensity is just our love for the challenge of competition. If I love to compete then that also means I'm going to love practice. That also means that I love the weight room. That also means that I love every part of the process because I love to compete and I love competition.

The second Pack Absolute is:
<u>Results are temporary, but your commitment to the team, The Pack, this ball club, this organization, this business... is forever</u>.
Results are very fleeting. People that tie themselves to results find out real quick that results will up and leave you. People that tie themselves to results are what I call emotional roller coasters. They're the guy that shows up and you don't know which guy you're getting on a certain day because it's always based off of how his results are going.

Results are temporary. Your commitment, your loyalty, your work ethic, your passion for this team is eternal.

Nobody is ever going to remember that you hit .340 as a senior. Nobody. The only people that will remember that you hit .340 as a senior are your Mama, your Daddy, and you. That's it. Your teammates certainly aren't going to remember that.

What your teammates will remember for a lifetime is your loyalty to them, your love for them, and your commitment to them. They will remember your passion. They will remember how hard you worked. They will remember how much you cared for them and how much you were willing to sacrifice for the greater good of this team.

Pack Absolute #3 comes out of *John 15:13*:

<u>There is no greater honor than to sacrifice for a brother.</u>

This program is founded on *John 15:13*. We are looking for guys that not only are willing to sacrifice for a brother but they <u>want</u> to sacrifice for a brother.

They say *"Pick me. Choose me. I will do that."* That is what we're looking for. We are looking for guys that will openly sacrifice for a brother.

The 4th Pack Absolute is:

The ability to grind.

We talked about what grind meant for us: *a continual pursuit to overachieve using the gifts that God has given you in any and all circumstances in order to obtain a desired outcome.*

Simply put, around here we embrace the suck. We embrace the grind. We embrace when it gets dirty. We embrace when it gets hard. We embrace going through adversity because it gives us a chance to respond.

This is what I want you to hear: **We embrace doing all of these things in silence**. Nobody wants to hear how bad you're hurting. Nobody wants to hear that you haven't played in a week. Those are energy vampires. Those are guys that suck the life out of the building.

Embrace the suck.
Embrace the grind.
Suffer in silence.

Nobody wants to hear you complain. **Either you're part of the problem or you're part of the solution.** Decide right now to be part of the solution, not part of the problem.

The 5th Pack Absolute

We play fast, hard, and loose in everything that we do.

We want you to play free. We want you to play unafraid to crash and burn. If you make a mistake, we want you to make that mistake going 1,000 miles per hour. We want you to make that mistake playing aggressively. We play fast, hard, and loose in Pack Baseball. That's the last thing I say before every time we take the field:

"Hey boys.. Play fast, hard, and loose.
Have fun!"

The 6th Pack Absolute is:

We want our guys to be extremely comfortable being uncomfortable.

We put our guys in situations, be it getting in a 45-50 degree swimming pool, making one team hit with a wooden bat while another team uses aluminum, putting one team in a five run disadvantage and saying, "I expect you to win this simulated game," putting one team on an 0-1 count and the other team on a 3-1 count all day… We put our guys in situations to embrace the grind, embrace the suck, suffer in silence, and to become extremely comfortable at being uncomfortable. At the end of the day when we're talking about offense, the entire thing is centered and based upon failure. With that failure, who has the ability to respond, respond the fastest, and continue to respond? That team or that guy holds a decisive advantage.

The 7th Pack Absolute is:

We punch the card.

We punch the timecard. We work. This is a program that is built on hard work. We have a saying around here: *"Hard work pays and guess what boys? Today is payday."*

Hard work pays off. There are no rewards passed out around here or anything else. It is an old school, blue-collar, old-fashioned formula where we roll up our sleeves, we punch the timecard, and we go to work. We take a tremendous amount of pride in outworking everybody.

We actually have a timecard machine that sits in our dugout, and everybody has a timecard, and we use that in game settings instead of the scoreboard to celebrate every little thing. Somebody wears a hit by pitch, somebody gets down the line, somebody leaves their feet, makes a great play, we score, have a pitcher go out and throw up a 0, anything that's in our control that we do a great job of... we punch that timecard.

We work and we accentuate that work by literally having a timecard with us on the field be it practice or in games.

The 8th Pack Absolute is the mindset that:

__It's only impossible until somebody does it.__
That is what this program lives by. If we were founded on *John 15:13*: *"No greater honor than to sacrifice for a brother,"* then what we live by is exactly like Jesus said in *Matthew 19:26*. He looked around and said, *"Yeah you're right, with man this would be impossible, but with God all things are possible."*

That is exactly what this program lives by. We truly believe that we are in the business of the impossible and that it's only impossible until somebody does it.

I want you to think about it in these terms:

Was anybody in the business of killing giants until 2000 years ago when David came along? No.

Was anybody in the business of going to the moon until NASA came along? No.

Was anybody in the business of beating the Russians in hockey until a bunch of misfits in 1980 came along? No.

It's only impossible until somebody does it. We are in the business of the impossible. **If you can see it, believe it, and outwork everybody for it, then at that moment you are in the business of the impossible.** Our mindset is that all things are possible.

The most important Pack Absolute is the most important thing you will ever do in your life:

Get up and respond.
We talked about intensity meaning wave after wave. I continue to talk about this because it is so important to give your guys opportunities to respond or to see when there is an opportunity to respond and bring that out in them. The most important thing you will ever do is make that business decision of getting back up. Wave after wave after wave... Just keep coming and keep getting

back up. Remember this: **We are never, ever, ever out of the fight.**

Those are the 9 Pack Absolutes. Remember this about The Pack Absolutes: **Whereas The Pack brings out your individuality, The Pack Absolutes are what we all do the same.** The Pack Absolutes are about being the absolute best at the stuff nobody else cares about. The Pack Absolutes are about being great at what we can control. The Pack Absolutes are about celebrating every single little small thing.

#1) Intensity allows us to overachieve.

#2) Results are temporary. Your commitment to team is forever.

#3) "There is no greater honor than to sacrifice for a brother."

#4) Embrace the grind. Embrace the suck. Suffer in silence.

#5) Play fast, hard, and loose.

#6) Be extremely comfortable at being uncomfortable.

#7) We punch the card, we work. There is no substitute for hard work. Hard work pays and today is payday.

#8) It is only impossible until somebody does it.

#9) You are never, ever out of the fight. I promise you that.

THE 5 PHASES OF BECOMING A PRODUCTIVE PACK MEMBER

The 5 Phases of Becoming a Productive Pack Member are, in essence, really the five phases of becoming a well-rounded man.

Our entire goal is to be able to play and live baggage free.

This baggage is not actual baggage. It's metaphorical baggage. We want to make sure that we're dotting i's, crossing t's, and that we're playing and living baggage free. We want to make sure that we deserve to win and that we deserve to be successful in every aspect of our life.

The five phases that I'm going to talk to you about today have to be in order in order for you to go on the mission with us. It's no different than a military member or a Navy SEAL or any other special operator. If things are not in order in their world or in their life, they can't go on the mission, and if they do, they're going to put other people in harm's way. They're going to put other people in jeopardy. We make sure that our guys are put in an incredible position to have success by mastering these five phases of their life. Like I mentioned earlier, it really boils down to the building of a well-rounded man.

All five of these phases feed off each other. Every one of these boxes needs to be checked because they feed off of each other either positively or negatively.

If one is neglected, it's going to hurt another area and then maybe another area, and it's ultimately going to trickle down into your performance at whatever you do. But if every box is checked, then all of these areas swirl around each other and it becomes a very powerful force and it creates a man that is ready to go out and have success in everything that he does.

The first phase I want to talk about with you is what we call **Mind, Body, Spirit**.

You have to make 100% sure that your mind, your body, and your spirit, are all on a full tank.

So let's start with our **mind**... We have to be very guarded, cautious, and aware of what we are feeding our mind and what is going into our mind. In today's day and age and especially with these young kids, think about all the things they have access to instantly. Are they feeding themselves with positive stuff or are they feeding themselves negative stuff? I want to be very aware of what I'm watching, what I'm listening to, and what I am hearing and what I am feeding into my mind. This is the #1 thing that you have. Keep yopur mind clear and sharp.

The second thing is my **body**...

We push these guys. These guys are all tremendous athletes. We've got to make sure that we're getting rested. We've got to make sure that we're staying hydrated. We've got to make sure that we're eating right with a great diet. This is all part of becoming a very successful man, professional athlete, whatever you want to call it...

The third part is our **spiritual life**...

I want to make sure that I am staying fed spiritually. Whatever you believe, you must be fed spiritually. If your spiritual tank is running on a quarter of a tank or it's running near empty, you are going to make some poor decisions personally, with your family, with your business decisions, and those three are going to swirl around each other.

We actively try to feed our guys – their mind, their body, and their spirit. We make sure that they're being fed and being fed the right things in all three of those areas. No matter what someone's beliefs are, any time you see a person hit some hard times, it's usually because they've made bad decisions that can generally be traced back to running on spiritual empty, not putting great stuff in their body, and putting trash in their mind.

So the first box we want to check is our mind, our body, and our spirit, and becoming an absolute professional at taking care of those three things and making sure that the tank is on full because when that tank is on full, we're going to make great decisions for our family, make great decisions personally, and we're going to make great business decisions.

The second phase to becoming a productive pack member are **relationships**.

The first thing is making sure that I'm maintaining the relationships that are already in my life, be it loved ones or really close friends. Those relationships need to be maintained and taken well care of. I have to do a great job in my relationships. If I neglect a relationship, I'm going to start to build baggage for myself.

We were built and we were made to be relational people. Great relationships can bring incredible energy and incredible joy to our lives. It is very wise and very smart to do a great job at maintaining the positive relationships that are already in your life.

Next with relationships is investing only in those that invest in you. I do not want to be a part of a relationship that is one sided. I want to make great decisions when it comes to the relationships that I have. **Nothing will ruin a career faster than a toxic relationship.** I only want to invest in those relationships that invest in me.

I want to make sure that I surround myself with those that are on the same mission as me. Remember what it says in Proverbs?

Iron sharpens iron.

I want to make sure that I am only investing in those that are on the same mission and have my best interest at heart. If I decide to take part in a toxic relationship, here's what's going to happen...

Where's it going to affect me first? It's going to affect my mind. Now we've created this vicious cycle where the relationship is now affecting the mind. Where is that going to go? It's going to go into my body, and then it's going to go right into my heart, so now it's affecting my spiritual side as well. I've got to be very diligent and very smart about my relationships.

The third phase in becoming a productive pack member is **appearance**.

I want to do an incredible job of taking care of what's been entrusted to me: my physical appearance. **My physical appearance is a first impression, and they say first impressions are everything, right?**

I want to make very sure that I'm doing a great job with my physical appearance. I want to be presentable. I want people when they see me to assume *"That guy is going in the right direction."*

If you walk in and you see me with my hat on backwards, and I'm in flip-flops with my shirt untucked, that's not going to put off a very good perception. I don't care who you are.

If you're neatly groomed, well dressed, have great poise, understand how to present yourself with humility, that is going to give off a great perception about you. Generally to do that, things need to be going pretty good with your mind, your body, your spirit, and your relationships.

That appearance trickles itself down into your apartment, your dorm room, your house, wherever you might live. It will trickle itself down into your vehicle. That appearance will trickle itself down into your locker, into your club house, into your field, your stadium, your dugout.

The first thing that we do when our guys get here every year – we don't practice, we don't condition – we spend a couple of days cleaning the facility. Why? Because that's ours. That has been entrusted to us and it's our appearance.

We have a no trash rule. If you see trash, you pick it up. It doesn't matter if it's on your way to your vehicle; it doesn't matter if it's on your way to the batter's box… Pick it up. Any dugout we ever visit, be it here or on the road, will be left better than we found it. There will be zero trash. Why? Because it's a reflection on us. It's our appearance.

Remember this:

Sloppy only breeds more sloppy.

When I look good – be it myself, my apartment, my vehicle, my locker, my clubhouse, my field, my dugout – when I look good, I'm more apt to play good and feel good. Besides that, it's just a pride thing. This is mine. We're going to take great care of it.

The 4th phase is **my responsibilities**.

You ask these guys, "What are your responsibilities right now?" Well your responsibility is to go to school, serve your community, get after it in the weight room, get after it in practice, become a great team, and go win championships. That's their job right now.

Like I said, there are no frills in this whole Pack deal. There are no rewards at the end or whatever... We work because that's what we're expected to do. We work. We punch the timecard and go back to work. We try to outwork everybody. So when it comes to your responsibilities, you have to go to work and stay on top of it.

We demand that our guys have 100% class attendance. They've got to sit in one of the first three rows. There's no hiding. They've got to participate in class. They've got to, at the end of each week, seek out their professor or instructor and present them with a comment or a question in order to build that relationship.

So many of the lessons in becoming a man are learning how to work and function in society. Learning how to network, getting that degree or passing classes isn't so much about being smart as it is about hard work, learning how to network, learning how to actively participate, learning how to show up, and figuring out a way to get it done.

The 5th phase of becoming a productive pack member is **having a grasp on your finances**.

I understand a lot of these guys (most of them) aren't paying their way through school, but it is never too early for them to start learning how to handle what they've worked for and what they've been blessed with and learning how to become a good steward over their finances. This is all part of becoming a well-rounded man. It's all part of living and playing baggage free.

We talk to our guys about saving. We talk to our guys about investing. We talk to our guys about living debt free. And then ultimately, we talk to these guys about giving back and learning to help those in need.

Nothing will ruin a relationship faster than finances. Nothing.

If our entire goal here as a program is to live and play baggage free, I want to walk through the gate every day baggage free. I can play unencumbered. I can play fast, hard, and loose. I'm not going to play fast, hard, and loose if I'm carrying baggage.

The mind, the body, and the spirit have to stay on a full tank. If the mind, body, and spirit aren't on a full tank, it's going to go into your relationships. If the relationships become toxic it's going to affect your appearance.

Do you see how it snowballs?

Do you see how it ultimately carries over into your job or responsibilities and your finances?

On the flip side of that, if you're checking the mind, body, spirit box and you're maintaining great relationships and you have a great appearance – be it with yourself, where you live, your vehicle, your locker space, your field, your dugout – you're going to be more apt to do an incredible job with your responsibilities. If you can learn to be a good steward over your finances, you're going to be able to check every one of these boxes and you are going to have mastery over *The 5 Phases of Being A Productive Pack Member*, of being a professional, of being a productive man.

THE PLAN OF ATTACK

We have been talking a lot about culture, team building, getting guys to overachieve, building a family, and so on...

This chapter is going to segue and take us more towards the baseball side of things...

The Plan of Attack for us is what we do on a daily basis. There are three things inside of The Plan of Attack. The Plan of Attack starts with what we call a takedown, and then we've got our four situations, and then we've got what we call Alpha ABs (at-bats). This goes from our early work into pre-practice, practice, conditioning... everything that we do is geared towards the Plan of Attack... every single little thing.

There is a definite method behind the madness of what we do and there is always a vision. It is so important when you work, when you practice, to have a vision, to have organization, to have – and we're back to this word again – clarity.

Clarity = Focus.

When you can have a singular focus, all bets are off. Anything is possible at that point. Obviously, there is a lot more that goes into it but that's where you want to start.

Our guys understand what we're attempting to do.

They understand where we're going.

They understand who we are.

They understand how we're going to get there.

A great way to make sure that your guys understand these concepts – this is oftentimes overlooked and I didn't understand this a lot as a young coach or leader – is to test your guys. No matter what business you're in, if it's baseball or if it's a corporation, test the guys. Literally test them. We do this a lot and this is all part of our Plan of Attack. When I say testing, I mean actual written tests. **Don't assume that somebody knows it until you test them.** Then after you grade that test, you may feel like not so great of a coach because it might prove to you that they don't truly understand what you guys are doing inside of your own plan of attack.

A great way to test guys is to test them in the nature of a game. So we'll pop them with a 10 question test and put a time limit on them. We'll stress them while they're taking the test, meaning there could be a lot of chaos, a lot of white noise (sometimes there's water involved, maybe), but we will stress them while they have to take this test. It goes back to becoming extremely comfortable at being uncomfortable. But you're not going to know that until you test those things.

Once everybody is done we'll grab the test and we'll ask The Pack to choose one test and they can't see it. They don't know whose name is on it. They'll pull it out of the stack and we'll take the rest of the stack and throw it in the trash. Now that one person is in the spotlight.

When you really think about it in the grand scheme of things, when it comes to athletics or business or anything else, when it comes to winning, it will always come down to one guy. **Passing is failing. Every test we take has to be 100%.** There will be a winner and loser of the test. It pays to be a winner in everything that you do.

Navy SEALs have a saying:

"You don't rise to the occasion, you always sink back to your level of training, so train well."

Essentially that's what we're doing. We're making sure that we've trained. We're testing them and we're seeing where we're at. We'll grade that one test, and it will come down to one guy and either he passes it or he fails it. If he fails it we'll pay it out. If he passes it, they all go nuts. This is just a great way to understand where you're at as a program and where your clarity is.

If you're disseminating this information or whatever your system is, test it. Test it weekly. Understand where you're at. Get a gauge of where you're at and where you're deficient. You have to check your ego at the door, humble yourself, and realize that – kind of like the drum beat example from chapter 1 – you may think they know, but they probably don't.

So under the Plan of Attack, we have one mission:

We want to make sure 100% that our opponent never forgets the day they played us.

I didn't say never forgets the scoreboard. I said we want to make sure they never forget the day they played us.

One of the greatest compliments I ever got as a coach was this: We got beat 10-0 one game and the head coach told me the next day, *"I honestly didn't know if we were winning or losing the entire time."* I said, *"Oh yeah, what do you mean?"* He said, *"Your guys never changed. I honestly thought we were losing at one point. I look up, it's 9-0."*

We never want our opponent to forget the day they had to play us. We want them to feel threatened. We want them to see our passion. We want them to understand that they are going to be in for an absolute dogfight. So now let's talk about the takedown…

We work on the takedown in various ways every single day. This at the core is who the Pack is. Inside of the takedown, **we do absolutely whatever it takes to score first.** It is vital that we score first. The team that scores first holds a gigantic advantage.

In 2014 when I was the hitting coach/recruiting coordinator at UL-Lafayette (a team that was 58-10), I believe we won every game that we scored first except for the last game of the year.

It is vital that we score first but what is more vital – this is where it gets lost in translation sometimes – is that when your opponent scores first, you are able to bounce back and respond. The best teams I've ever had when our opponent scores, say they scored 2, we respond and come in and score 4.

We call it **jabs vs. haymakers**. You throw a jab at us, you're getting a haymaker. It literally excites these guys when somebody scores first on us. They don't drop their head. It angers them. We've conditioned these guys to respond.

Let's go through the takedown...

We score first. Once we score first (this is what we call in our verbiage house money whenever we've scored first), now what we're going to do is start shortening the field on you. To shorten the field for us means using our short game. It means creating chaos, being a distraction on the bases, starting to run. We are going to start to shorten the field on you once we've scored first, once we've got house money.

That field is going to start to get shortened, and when that field starts to get shortened, there's an opposite effect as well. Now mistakes start to happen and the field starts to get lengthened back out so you get the best of both worlds. Before you know it, you look up and there's a meeting going on at the mound, maybe the pitcher is looking at the dugout. Maybe there is a meeting with the whole team after we hit that inning.

We actually keep track of how many meetings we can induce. Our guys take pride in that stuff because we understand now that we've scored first that we've got house money. So we're looking to shorten the field and then lengthen the field back out, and now the game is starting to slowly but surely spin out of control on our opponent.

Now the game is spinning. It's real fast for our opponent right now. You have to take advantage of opponent's mistakes. You have to tax the guy on the bump and you've got to tax the defense. When you can do that, you're invariably going to make your way into that bullpen, and when you make your way into the bullpen, go trash the joint. You want to make an absolute mess of that place. Go trash the bullpen and do what we call knock them all the way into Sunday. Knock them all into Sunday is code for this: They've played us once, make them not want to be here anymore. That's the takedown and that's what we work on every single day. If you don't score first, you better make sure you have enough gumption and guts to respond.

The second part of the Plan of Attack is something I came up with years ago to simplify things. It's very pertinent into how we play the game. It takes a while to teach. It's a tough teach, but it will save you. It's called the four situations. So everything we do offensively or defensively is always predicated on the four situations. Everything we do. Above and beyond that, it's predicated off of this: pitcher, catcher, scoreboard. Anything I ever do in a game ever will always first go to me understanding who is pitching, who is catching, and what's the score.

I'll put it in perspective for you. If Pudge Rodriguez is catching and Andy Pettitte is pitching (one of the best pick off moves of all time, if not the best) and I'm down by 5, that's going to severely limit my takedown. If I flip the script though and I've got Andy Pettitte pitching for me and Pudge Rodriguez catching and we're up by 5, it's also going to enhance the takedown. No matter who you have or who you're facing, you always have to answer those three questions first: pitcher, catcher, scoreboard.

That takes me into these four situations. Be it offensively or defensively, we have four spots in which we play the game. This sets the tempo of how we play. It avoids a lot of confusion. It avoids a lack of clarity, and it answers how we play without ever saying a word in a particular spot. But it always goes back to practice. You have to work the takedown. You have to work the Plan of Attack inside the Pack Offense or Pack Defense.

We have a sign for all four of these situations. A lot of times we don't have to give the sign because we've conditioned our guys to know instantly pitcher, catcher, scoreboard and what situation we're in based off that.

The first situation that we play in is **on fire**.

On fire for us is the way we start or finish every game when given the opportunity. What I mean by that is if we come out in a 0-0 game, we're looking to throw the first lick. It is a blitzkrieg. No baseball rules – and this is the teach – no baseball rules apply. What is a baseball rule? Don't make first or third out at third. That's out the window. Don't swing 3-0. That's out the window. No baseball rules apply for us. This is fast, hard, and loose. We're looking to jump into that feeding frenzy immediately. You know the old Mike Tyson saying *"Everybody's got a game plan until they get punched in the mouth?"* We're looking to do the punching in the mouth right here.

(On the other side of that, you've got to build a team that is strong enough to get punched in the mouth and respond.)

We start every game on fire and it's how we finish up five or more runs. Think of it in these terms. Visualize this. You go for a hustle double or you steal that bag or you read that ball in the dirt. It's going to be a bang-bang play and there is a chance that you're going to be out... or you're looking to auto swing at the dish 3-0 and you get that chest high cookie and get that swing off.

There's risk involved in playing on fire, but it is backyard baseball at it's finest. Everybody has been there with that wiffle ball game or tennis ball game or whatever it might be, and it is the loosest, freest, fastest you've ever played. That's the state we try to get these guys in to start a game, when up by 5, and to finish a game. A lot of it is a perception.

Second situation: Hot.

Hot for us means you're either the winning or tying run or we're up by four or less. **We are playing to win in a hot situation.** Back to the aggressor thing... So many people in a winning or tying run scenario play what? They play not to lose. No. I understand this already... With one out, I want to be at third. With zero or two outs, I want to be at second. With two outs in a tied game and I hit a tweener ball over the shortstop's head, my guy better be involved in a bang-bang play at second base trying to get in scoring position because he already knew he's in a hot situation. He's already been schooled on that and understands that.

My guy understands that in a tie game – because winning, tying run, or up by four or less, we're hot – that if he's at second base with one out and he gets a dirt ball read opportunity, where had he better be involved in a bang bang play? Third base.

I know we've got to be at second with zero or two outs, or at third base with one out.

Our entire offense is predicated around one thing: **runner at third base less than two outs.** We will double to triple our opponents in that stat every year.

So we've got on fire, we've got hot, and now we get into our third situation:

Lukewarm

Lukewarm is an interesting scenario. I want you to think about lukewarm like this: It means we're losing by 3-4 runs in the middle of the game. Those are lukewarm scenarios. So 3rd-6th inning with a 3-4 run deficit. That's a lukewarm scenario. We use a flashing yellow light. That's the way I want you to think about lukewarm inside of our four situations. We've got a sign for these because we don't want mistakes being made at crucial parts of the game based off our offense, our baserunning, or our defense. So lukewarm means I'm going to use a caution sign. It means I will advance. It's no different than a yellow light. I will advance but there is a dang near 100% chance I'm going to make it. I'll take the extra base. I'll get my swing off, but it's going to be in a good count. I'll leave my feet in the outfield but it's going to be smart. Ideally in that lukewarm spot, I want to keep adding base runners offensively because I'm trailing 3-4 runs in the middle of the game. Use a yield sign. Do not run into outs. Do not wreck an inning right there.

Our 4th situation is this: **cold**.

Cold means we are losing big early, losing big middle, or we're down by two or more late. That's cold. The only way I swing is after I've seen a strike. The only way I advance is if I know I can go in standing up. We're looking to play station to station in this scenario.

We're playing station to station baseball. Our objective in this spot right here – and we've done it many times – is to load the bases and hit for 30 minutes. That's our best way back into the game. The goal is to avoid weak early outs and to avoid dumb mistakes on the bases. We understand pitcher, catcher, scoreboard, the score is 5-0. That's a cold situation for us.

The 4 Situations
On Fire – how we start or how we finish you when given the opportunity

Hot – winning, tying run, up by four or less. We are the aggressor, unafraid to crash and burn in that spot.

Lukewarm – flashing yellow light, down 3-4 middle of the game

Cold – down five or more early, five or more middle, and then by two or more late... We need base runners. We need great decisions.

Now I'm going to give you a for instance right here with the takedown and our four situations...

How did I say we start every game? On fire. So leadoff batter. Flare over the shortstop's head. I know he wants to be aware with no outs. Where had he better get? Second base. We're fine with him being thrown out at second base because we want to make that statement. We want to throw that first lick. They know what they're getting into. We want to give it to them. He gets a hustle double because we're on fire and he knows with no outs, he wants to be at second base.

But inside of the takedown what's our mission? We already said it. What do we want to do? We will do absolutely whatever it takes to what? Score first. So here's where your situations come in. All of a sudden, we were on fire to start the game. Now he's at second and he looks at me at third and I let him know what? He's cold. Why is he cold? Because it goes back to the takedown. The situation comes back into the takedown. The takedown says we're going to score first. Our guys already know because we practice this every day… The next guy is drag bunting for a hit. He's going to third, so he goes cold.

We're not making the first out at 3rd. Now he's at 3rd with one out, and I've already told you that's our bread and butter. We will set that situation up 2-3x more than our opponent every year. Now we're at 3rd base, and we're back to being hot. Now it's time for an Alpha AB.

That's the third part of the Plan of Attack:
Alpha ABs

These are at-bats with a runner at 3rd base and less than two outs. The whole premise of the pack offense revolves around scoring a run in an inning by getting that runner to third base with less than two outs – an Alpha AB.

The way we approach Alpha ABs is like a street fight mentality. I know that in a street fight mentality the guy that throws the first lick has way better odds. Our odds with this runner at 3rd base – we call it our bread and butter – need to sit at 70% or higher. That's what we practice. I know I'm going to throw the first lick. I cannot tell you how much you need to practice this spot. I cannot tell you how important it is to not let the pitcher use you against you.

There are three things in this spot that the pitcher wants in this order: he wants a rollover to a corner, he wants a popup in the infield, or if he gets you down on your back, he wants to punch you out.

We have a couple of rules in this spot. #1 is that we know we want 70% success in driving that run in. Well, to drive that run in 9 times out of 10, it doesn't take a hit because they're going to play their middle infield back, so I am hunting low and hard middle of the field. Say I'm a right-handed hitter... I'm hunting low and hard at that second baseman. Left-handed hitter... I'm hunting low and hard at the shortstop. I'm going to take the plate away. I'm going to be late and short hunting low and hard and I want to get it done early. Back to that street fight thing. I want to throw the first lick.

Our rules, hard and fast, are that we're not taking a strike with a runner at third and less than two. Not going to do it. A lot of times what are they going to do? They're going to try to use you against you. They're going to try to elevate a curve ball for strike one. Why am I going to take an elevated breaking ball for strike one? If my hands are back I can sink into that front side, hit me a ground ball line drive up the middle or the other way and I've got a steak. I've got a ribeye. We're on the board. We've scored first.

See how it takes us back into the takedown? We've scored first.

Now we have what? House money.

Now it's time to:
Shorten.
Lengthen.
Spin.
Feeding frenzy.

It's all tied together... on fire, leadoff double, bam. Cold. Base lead. Alright. Drag bunt to move him over. Now we got runner at third base with one out. Pitcher tries to land a first pitch hanger and get ahead of me, but bam, I'm hunting up the middle, low and hard other way. Now we're on the board. That's a mature Alpha AB.

An amateur AB would be me key holing this guy looking for one pitch to hit a double. I don't need a double. I just need to rake in every time there's a guy at third and one out. I already know from the history of our offense that there's going to be a ton of guys at third base with one out. Take advantage of every opportunity.

The second type of Alpha AB is this: **a runner at second base, two outs**.

Big hit. Our hard and fast rule right here is this: we are not taking strike two. We will not take strike two in that spot. This goes back to the aggressor always wins. I'll give you a pitch or two because it's going to take a base hit to drive this guy in from second. Two out knocks are back breakers. They're crushing.

Those are the things that make guys not want to be out there anymore. Scoring with two outs, that stuff takes heart, and it takes guys that plays with a passion to be able to score with two outs and nothing going. Can't take strike two. We'll give you strike one. You get down a little bit we need to start thinking base knock middle of the field. Stay the aggressor in that spot. Don't let this guy get on top of you and put you in a negative count because you're key holing him. That's being an amateur hitter. Get in there ready to hit. Guys that drive in runs swing the bat. Make that guy not want to be out there anymore. That's how you win championships, two out knocks, extending innings...

Those are Alpha ABs.
That's how you win.

The Takedown, the 4 Situations, and our Alpha Abs make up **The Plan of Attack**. We work at them every day.

If you haven't heard anything I want you to hear this: **I am the hunter. He is the hunted**.

Our mission every day inside The Plan of Attack is to **make sure the other team always remembers the day they had to play The Pack.**

About The Author

Matt Deggs is a college baseball coach, author, and speaker.

Deggs, who for years was a transactional coach that only lived for himself, was addicted to alcohol and consequently destroyed a career, family and countless relationships along the way. He now is a changed man.

Going from bearing bad fruit or little to no fruit at all, Deggs has seen his life come full circle and now strives to live a life full of service, impact, development and bearing good fruit not only in his life but in the lives of his family, friends and players.

Deggs by the grace of God is married to his wife Kathy and they have 3 children: Kyler, Klaire, and Khloe...

Coaching is only part of what Deggs does now. He also speaks to churches, groups, companies and other men & coaches... not only of his journey and testimony, but also in the fields of leadership, team building & transformational coaching.

Deggs has been to the highest of highs and the lowest lows and has found a way to climb all the way back... His life has been one of blessing, tragedy and triumph; a life of defying odds and battling back.

15 to 28

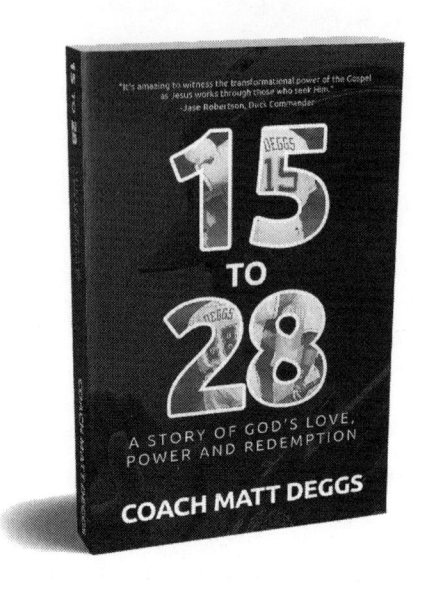

15 to 28 is a riveting story that reveals God's love, power, and redemption through 28 true stories from the life of Coach Matt Deggs. His journey in (and out) of college baseball is a true testament to what is possible when we remove ourselves from the equation and let God work in us.

Visit
CoachDeggs.com/Book
to get your copy today!

The Pack Video System

Throughout this online video program, you will uncover the foundation of what has helped Coach Deggs' lead record-breaking teams.

The Pack Video System includes **nearly 3 hours** of Coach Deggs' teaching his proven formula to building teams with strong identity, clear purpose, and unbreakable culture.

Visit
CoachDeggs.com/Pack
to learn more and get started today!

Speaking

Coach Deggs delivers **keynote and transformational speaking engagements** to leaders, athletic teams, churches, and corporate organizations across the country.

Visit

CoachDeggs.com/Speaking

to book Coach Deggs to speak at your next event!

Made in the USA
Columbia, SC
18 February 2020